ÌMAGES
of America

VENTURA COUNTY
VETERANS
WORLD WAR II TO VIETNAM

OUR DEBT TO THE HEROIC MEN AND VALIANT WOMEN IN THE SERVICE OF OUR COUNTRY CAN NEVER BE REPAID. THEY HAVE EARNED OUR UNDYING GRATITUDE. AMERICA WILL NEVER FORGET THEIR SACRIFICES.

PRESIDENT HARRY S TRUMAN

A TRIBUTE. A fitting quote by Pres. Harry Truman is displayed as part of the World War II Memorial in Washington, DC—lest Americans forget. (Courtesy Mike De Los Santos, Camarillo.)

ON THE COVER: On May 6, 1942, Lawrence Frost (far left and behind fold) and his brother Clair (second from left) were taken as prisoners of war by the Japanese on Corregidor Island. More than 11,500 American and Filipino troops who survived the battle were also taken as prisoners. This photograph was taken after Frost and five others returned home from being held captive for more than three years. Both Lawrence and his brother Clair were from Oxnard. (Courtesy of Lawrence Frost.)

IMAGES
of America

VENTURA COUNTY
VETERANS
WORLD WAR II TO VIETNAM

Jannette Jauregui

ARCADIA
PUBLISHING

Published by Arcadia Publishing
Charleston, South Carolina

Printed in the United States of America

Library of Congress Control Number: 2010941635

For all general information, please contact Arcadia Publishing:
Telephone 843-853-2070
Fax 843-853-0044
E-mail sales@arcadiapublishing.com
For customer service and orders:
Toll-Free 1-888-313-2665

Visit us on the Internet at www.arcadiapublishing.com

This book is dedicated to all hometown heroes. We, as a nation, are forever indebted to you for your selfless service. May you always be remembered.

CONTENTS

ACKNOWLEDGMENTS

First and foremost, my undying gratitude is extended to the veterans of Ventura County who have so graciously welcomed me into their lives to share a portion of their stories. You have all touched my life in ways no words can describe, and I continue to be honored to know each one of you.

Credit is given to Marianne Ratcliff and the *Ventura County Star* and to Don and Debbie Johnson and the *Santa Paula Times* for giving a 19-year-old aspiring journalist a shot at being published. Also, thanks go to John Nichols for your artistic support over the years. Your guidance has been priceless.

To Arcadia Publishing: My deepest thanks for giving me the opportunity to pay tribute to some of Ventura County's finest.

I thank my parents, Joe and Wannette Jauregui, for their support and encouragement as I do things "my way."

Lastly, I have special remembrance for Tony Vasquez Sr. and Hector Borrego, for teaching me about courage and heroism in life and death.

Unless otherwise noted, all images used in this book come from the personal collections of each veteran and their family.

INTRODUCTION

For more than 10 years, I have been documenting and sharing the stories of many of Ventura County's veterans as part of my column for the *Ventura County Star*, "Of War and Life." During the years that I have gotten to know our hometown heroes, I have come to admire and respect them both as individuals and as former members of this country's armed forces.

In Ventura County, the military service of its residents dates back to wars that were fought even before cities in the area were officially established. Santa Paula, for example, was incorporated in 1902. However, its cemetery holds the bodies of residents who served in the Civil War and Spanish-American War.

For a fairly small region, with a total population of approximately 800,000 residents, the number of veterans residing in the county today is immense.

As of December 2010, there were approximately 60,000 veterans living in Ventura County. Some are native to the area, and others came to call it home later in life.

Their stories are all unique, from the Hawaiian shores and the battleships of Pearl Harbor, to the African coast, battles in Sicily, into Northern France and Germany, and also the battle stations in the Pacific, to South Korea, and the jungles of Vietnam. In each location, a Ventura County veteran's story can be found.

Some served multiple years and multiple tours. Some were drafted, while others volunteered. All served honorably.

There are those who protected the home front with stateside service. There are families who sent two or three, sometimes even four, sons to war. And there are the fathers who fought in World War II, who hoped their children would never have to endure the horrors of war, and the sons who followed their footsteps in Vietnam. There were the childhood friends that boarded the buses to boot camp together. And there are those who gave the ultimate sacrifice, laying down their lives on foreign lands, leaving behind families and friends with a devastating loss. Some of their bodies were never recovered.

The combat and life experiences of the men and women included in this book are vast. They fought on the ground, in the air, and at sea. Many were prisoners of war.

Each story I have been told includes this question: "Why did I make it home when so many others were killed and left behind?" It is a question that seems to haunt every combat veteran.

One story that has remained at the forefront of my mind came from the first veteran interview I conducted. In the spring of 2001, I interviewed Tony Vasquez, a World War II veteran from Santa Paula. In sharing his story, he told me of the battles he fought throughout Europe, of his shrapnel wounds, and of his time of mistreatment as a prisoner of war (POW). Though those experiences alone would merit negativity and nightmares, it was another part of his story that haunted him instead.

Gregory Vera, a 19-year-old Californian, was Vasquez's first runner. While in combat just outside of Normandy, France, Vasquez sent Vera to relay a message to their captain. Vera never returned. Vasquez soon learned that he, along with the captain, had been killed. Vasquez blamed himself for Vera's death, telling me that he should have been the one to relay the message. That way Vera might have had the chance to come home.

Vasquez never knew if Vera's body was recovered and buried. It was not until 2007, when I traveled to the Normandy American Cemetery and found Vera's headstone that Vasquez finally found some peace. Vasquez's story is one of many that, since his death in 2009, are no longer available firsthand.

In the fall of 2006, I received a letter from Ed Weigel, a World War II veteran from Oxnard. He asked if I would be interested in interviewing him about his combat experiences. I filed the letter inside a notebook in which I had been collecting letters and e-mails. Like every other letter and e-mail, I planned to get to it as soon as I could. Unbeknownst to me, Weigel was fighting a losing battle with cancer. In January 2007, I called his home to schedule an interview and his wife told me that he had passed away only weeks before. It was a wake-up call I was not prepared for.

Each year, the number of World War II, Korean War, and Vietnam veterans that pass away only grows, and the stories that were never told die with them. As a nation, I believe it is our responsibility to collect as many stories as possible, starting with our families, neighbors, and friends.

This book is my way of paying tribute to some of those stories.

In my quest to collect photographs, I reached out to veterans in Ventura County via newspapers, church bulletins, meetings, letter writing, and quite simply, by word of mouth. Unfortunately, I was not able to include each photograph that was submitted. Though there are countless of veterans from Ventura County that are not accounted for in this book, it is my hope that this record of local military service will serve as a representation of the region's heroes—men and women who gave themselves to serve our country in the name of freedom.

One

WORLD WAR II

881ST ENGINEER AVIATION BATTALION reservists include, from left, standing, Pfc. Joe C. Correa, Santa Barbara; Pfc. Lynn D. Box, Oak View; Sgt. Orral L. Mauzer, Ojai; Cpl. Donald Harrington, Ventura; Cpl. Dalles C. Tester, Oxnard; kneeling, Sgt. Colver H. Jones, Camarillo; Sgt. 1/c Clifford B. Perry, Ojai; M/Sgt. George M. Hawkins, Oxnard; and Cpl. Waide R. Hammer, Ventura.
—Army Photo

RESERVISTS OF THE 881ST ENGINEER AVIATION BATTALION. The group poses during their service at the close of World War II. Pictured from left to right are (kneeling) Colver H. Jones, Camarillo; Sfc. Clifford B. Perry, Ojai; M.Sgt. George M. Hawkins, Oxnard; and Cpl. Waide R. Hammer, Ventura; (standing) Pfc. Joe C. Correa, Santa Barbara; Pfc. Lynn D. Box, Oak View; Sgt. Orral L. Mauzer, Ojai; Cpl. Donald Harrington, Ventura; and Cpl. Dallas C. Tester, Oxnard. (Courtesy of Evelyn Tester.)

DALLAS TESTER. The Oxnard man poses during a break from training at Fort Leonard Wood, Missouri. Tester served in the Army from March 1943 to December 1945. (Courtesy of Evelyn Tester.)

FRANK ARELLANO. Pvt. Frank Arellano of Santa Paula served in Japan with the Eighth Army from December 1945 to June 1946. When he was 31 years old, he received an honorable discharge on July 17, 1946. (Courtesy of Frank Arellano.)

BENNIE JEW. Bennie Jew of Ojai takes a break to pose for a photograph in the fall of 1944. He was completing flight training at the Lodwick School of Aeronautics in Lakeland, Florida, where, soon after, he met his wife, Cora. (Courtesy of Bennie Jew.)

A B-52 CREW. The group gathers during combat training at Castle Air Force Base, California. Bennie Jew, who is pictured on the far left, continued his Air Force career well beyond World War II. This photograph was taken in the summer of 1960, which was shortly after the crew was assigned to the 28th Bomb Wing at Ellsworth Air Force Base near Rapid City, South Dakota. The crew went on to fly 51 bombing missions over South Vietnam. (Courtesy of Bennie Jew.)

BILLYE GRYMWADE. In 1944, Ventura resident Grymwade enlisted in the WAVES, a World War II–era division of the Navy that consisted entirely of women. She said of her decision to enlist, "I must confess that when I enlisted, I had no great shakes feelings of patriotism. Just wanted to get out of town. But the day I first put on the uniform, after alterations were done, the feeling of patriotism washed over me like a wave." (Courtesy of Billye Grymwade.)

ANDY ANGUIANO. Ventura resident Anguiano served as a "BAR man" in the 45th Infantry Division in North Africa and Sicily. The name of his gun was an acronym for Browning Automatic Rifle (BAR). Anguiano also served in the 5th Army Division throughout Europe. He was wounded during the invasion of Salerno and eventually received a Purple Heart and Silver Star medal for his combat efforts. (Courtesy Andy Anguiano.)

EDUCATOR AT WAR.
George McNeely
was working as an
instructor at Ventura
College when Pearl
Harbor was bombed.
He once said, "Most
of my students were
gone as part of the
draft, so I figured I
should go along, too."
McNeely served as a
member of the Navy
through the D-Day
invasion in June
1944. (Courtesy of
George McNeely.)

JOE CASAS. The Santa Paula man was
drafted into the Army in April 1943.
He fought in the Battle of Okinawa in
1945. Journalist Ernie Pyle, who covered
the battle, described the soldiers he
met with the following statement:
"They have fears, and qualms and
hatred for the war, the same as anybody
else. They want to go home as badly
as any soldier I've ever met." The
noted journalist was killed in combat
soon after. (Courtesy of Joe Casas.)

13

SERVICE ALONGSIDE CAMELOT. Fred Stewart, who was from Santa Paula, poses while on leave in December 1943. Soon after, he was deployed to the Philippines where he served the remainder of the war. As part of his duty, Stewart worked as an instructor and taught PT boat handling alongside former president John F. Kennedy. (Courtesy of Charles Stewart.)

JOHN STOCKDILL. The former Santa Paula High School teacher enlisted in the Navy immediately after graduating from high school in 1942. He served as a carpenter's mate throughout the Pacific, including in Hollandia, New Guinea. Describing the moment when he landed in Hollandia, Stockdill said, "It was a bloody mess still, and there were bodies still floating around and on shore that hadn't been recovered." (Courtesy of John Stockdill.)

HENRY "JR." KREIGER. In the spring of 1944, Fillmore native Kreiger enlisted in the Army just a few months before his 18th birthday. Kreiger served with the 44th Infantry Division in France and Germany. (Courtesy of Henry Kreiger.)

ERNIE MANALIO. The proud Italian American was drafted into the Army in 1942 and served at military hospitals stateside. The Thousand Oaks man provided entertainment and emotional support to combat troops returning from overseas. (Courtesy of Ernie Manalio.)

A WAVE. Marie Connelly Gallicchio of Ventura enlisted as a WAVE in August 1944. She trained as a surgical nurse and eventually served at the hospital on the marine base at Quantico, Virginia. (Courtesy of Marie Connelly Gallicchio.)

DARREL LARSEN. Larsen enlisted in the Army Air Corps in November 1942 at 20 years old. Originally from Ventura, he served in the Eighth Air Force as an engineer gunner aboard a B-24. His missions included bombing raids before and during the D-Day invasion on June 6, 1944. (Courtesy of Darrel Larsen.)

USS FANNING. Taken in February 1945, Emmett Quady is pictured on the forward main deck of the USS *Fanning* in Saipan Harbor. He served as a gunnery officer and eventually received a Bronze Star medal for his combat contributions in the Pacific. Quady was from Westlake Village. (Courtesy Scott Quady.)

EVA PINKHAM. Ojai resident Pinkham enlisted in the WAVES on November 27, 1943. She trained as a nurse and served at Mare Island Hospital in California, tending to wounded troops who returned from combat in the Pacific. She went on to serve at Base Eight near Barbers Point on Oahu, Hawaii. (Courtesy Eva Pinkham.)

NAVY NURSE. Erma Lucille Ball from Port Hueneme enlisted in the Navy in 1941. She served as an ensign nurse in San Diego and San Francisco until she was discharged in August 1945. (Courtesy of Duane Rich.)

1ST AIR COMMANDO. Charles Campbell of Thousand Oaks was a member of the 1st Air Commandos led by Lt. Col. Philip Cochran. Campbell flew missions throughout China, Burma, and India, including the hazardous nighttime invasion of northern Burma dubbed "Operation Broadway" in March 1944. (Courtesy of Charles Campbell.)

JOHN GARDNER. Oxnard resident Gardner survived three years of combat in Europe before he was 21 years old. He was drafted into the Army on February 17, 1943, which was his 19th birthday. His proudest accomplishment was flying 30 missions without losing a single member of his crew. He said of his crew, "They were more than a crew. They were my family." (Courtesy of John Gardner.)

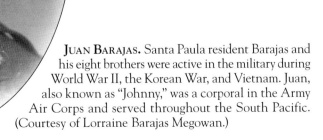

JUAN BARAJAS. Santa Paula resident Barajas and his eight brothers were active in the military during World War II, the Korean War, and Vietnam. Juan, also known as "Johnny," was a corporal in the Army Air Corps and served throughout the South Pacific. (Courtesy of Lorraine Barajas Megowan.)

AERIAL PHOTOGRAPHER. Camarillo resident Ken Nelson enlisted in the Army Air Corps in 1942 and served as part of the 100th Bomb Group that flew B-17s. He was also part of the 462nd Bomb Group as an aerial photographer aboard a B-29. Prior to his service in the Army Air Corps, Nelson served in the National Guard, a role he held at just 16 years old. (Courtesy of Ken Nelson.)

CIVILIAN CONSERVATION CORPS. Santa Paula resident Lyle Gunderson worked for the Civilian Conservation Corps in Minnesota from 1939 until he enlisted in the Army on December 10, 1940. He was sent on active duty to Anchorage, Alaska, to help build and fortify Fort Richardson. From there, with the United States struggling in Europe, Gunderson was sent to Chaffee, Arkansas, for artillery training before landing in France on September 26, 1944. (Courtesy Virginia Richardson Gunderson.)

ARMY MEDIC. Jess Victoria, along with brothers Manuel, Joe, and Rudy, were sent to war from their hometown of Santa Paula. Jess served as a medic in the Pacific, including battles in New Guinea and the Philippines. (Courtesy of Jess Victoria.)

WAR BRIDE. Ventura resident Marie Hodges, shown here on her wedding day with her husband and American Seabee, Marvin Hodges, served as a messenger with the Royal Navy. She moved to the United States with her husband when World War II ended. (Courtesy of Marie Hodges.)

WEDDING DAY. Ventura resident Jack Smith is pictured in uniform on his wedding day with his wife, Marie Jauregui Smith. Smith served in the Navy. The couple got married in St. Augustine Cathedral in Tucson, Arizona. Smith went on to teach and coach at Ventura High School. (Courtesy of Joe Jauregui.)

ARMY IN HIS BLOOD. On August 2, 1943, Gordon Welsh (left) followed in his father's footsteps by enlisting in the Army. The Santa Paula resident was assigned to the 26th Infantry Division. Soon after he swore in, Welsh boarded a troop transport ship headed to France. On November 18, 1944, while in combat, Welsh was shot in the arm by German artillery. He was sent back to the United States for treatment and was discharged on September 7, 1945. (Courtesy of Gordon Welsh.)

JAMES BROOKS. Santa Paula resident Brooks (far right) is pictured with members of his squad on their last day of combat in 1945. He was sent to Europe in May 1944 and participated in the D-Day invasion, landing on Utah Beach. He continued to fight throughout France, Belgium, Holland, and Germany. (Courtesy of James Brooks.)

CARL BARRINGER. The Santa Paula man enlisted as an Army Reserve in the summer of 1942. He was called to active duty in April 1943 and eventually joined Terry Allen's 104th Infantry Division. He deployed to France in September 1944 and saw his first battle in October in Holland. This photograph was taken on April 21, 1945, in Delitzsch, Germany. (Courtesy Carl Barringer.)

Tutsomo "Ben" Taketa. For several years after the bombing of Pearl Harbor, Japanese Americans were often looked down upon. Because of that, many were not given the opportunity to fight on the front lines. For this reason, Tutsomo "Ben" Taketa of Santa Paula served as a cook with the 442nd Division in Oklahoma and Italy. (Courtesy of Virginia Richardson Gunderson.)

California National Guard. Ventura resident Ambrose Little enlisted in the California National Guard in 1939 and was inducted into federal service on October 22, 1940. He was, at the time, stationed in Fort Lewis, Washington, but was moved to California for coast artillery duty after the bombing of Pearl Harbor in December 1941. Little went on to serve as a sergeant mechanic in charge of maintaining 15 M4 high-speed prime movers in France. (Courtesy of Ambrose Little.)

GLORIA NOBLE. The Ventura resident Noble (left) enlisted as a WAVE on May 31, 1944. She worked as a telegrapher and was assigned to the 11th Naval District based out of Point Loma, San Diego. (Courtesy of Gloria Noble.)

THEIR DAY IN MAY. Ventura residents Walter and Jean Weidenfeller met while he was on a 30-day leave from the Navy. They spent each day together, and when it was time for Walter to leave, the couple promised themselves to one another. They were married on May 19, 1941. Walter was eventually assigned to duty in Pearl Harbor and was there on the morning of December 7, 1941, when the Japanese bombed the American military bases. (Courtesy of Walter and Jean Weidenfeller.)

A Canadian Soldier. Thousand Oaks resident William Ferguson, a former member of the Royal Regiment of Canada, was one of 200 men taken as a prisoner of war (POW) while fighting in the Battle of Dieppe in August 1942. Within days, more than half of the prisoners were dead because of cold temperatures and illnesses that ran rampant during their rigorous marches and on the farm where the POWs eventually settled. (Courtesy of Drew Ferguson.)

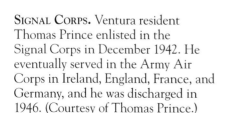

Signal Corps. Ventura resident Thomas Prince enlisted in the Signal Corps in December 1942. He eventually served in the Army Air Corps in Ireland, England, France, and Germany, and he was discharged in 1946. (Courtesy of Thomas Prince.)

TIM SANTANA. Santa Paula resident Santana was inducted into the Army on November 14, 1944. He was assigned to the 8th Cavalry Regiment in Manila Bay in May 1945 and was ordered on combat patrols against the Japanese. When the war ended in August 1945, Santana was sent to occupation duty in Japan. This photograph was taken in Salinas, California, in 1946—the year he received his honorable discharge. (Courtesy of Tim Santana.)

JAMES SATTERFIELD. Fillmore resident Satterfield did not think twice about enlisting in the Army when he heard the Japanese attacked the Pacific Fleet in Pearl Harbor. He enlisted as a member of the Army Air Corps and served with the 45th Bombardment Squadron, completing maintenance work on various aircraft and as a tail gunner. His maintenance duties included work on the newly released B-29 Superfortress. (Courtesy of James Satterfield.)

NEBRASKA NATIONAL GUARD. In October 1940, Ventura resident Verl Carpenter joined the Nebraska National Guard to earn a little extra money while attending college. He was called to active duty when the war began and served with the 134th Infantry Regiment in combat throughout France. On October 12, 1944, Carpenter was wounded in the leg by German artillery in Manhoue, France. (Courtesy of Verl Carpenter.)

ARTHUR SEIFERT. Camarillo resident Seifert served in the Signal Corps from July 16, 1943, to October 1945. He was assigned to the 305th Signal Operation Battalion and was in combat throughout Europe, including the Battle of Bulge in 1944. Here, Seifert is pictured on the left with his war buddy John Sotak in Verdun, France, in August 1944. (Courtesy of Leslie Seifert-De Los Santos.)

DAVID DRAPEAU. Ventura resident Drapeau enlisted in the Navy on June 6, 1942, while attending Ventura Community College. He remained enrolled in courses until July 1, 1943, when he was sent to Navy Supply Corps training at Wellesley College. He served as a supply officer aboard the USS *Sierra* throughout the Pacific. Drapeau went on to practice law in Ventura, eventually becoming a judge. (Courtesy of Beverly Drapeau.)

FRANK COVELLO. Oak Park resident Covello was one of six siblings to fight in World War II. He was sent to the South Pacific and fought in Leyte and Peleliu. Covello later served occupational duty in Japan. He was sent home to the United States in early 1946. (Courtesy of Frank Covello.)

GLENN GOOSS. Ventura resident Gooss's time in the Army began on December 24, 1942. He was a first lieutenant with the 29th Infantry Division and the platoon leader of a rifle squad, serving throughout Europe until the end of the war in 1945. This photograph was taken in Bremen, Germany, during occupation of the country. (Courtesy of Glenn Gooss.)

USS PRINCETON. On October 24, 1944, the Ojai resident William Hansen Jr. was serving aboard the USS *Princeton* when the ship was sunk by a Japanese dive-bomber. Hansen and his shipmates were picked up by the USS *Irwin.* Later, he was assigned duty aboard the USS *Bairoko* and was discharged in February 1946. (Courtesy of Lois Hansen.)

JACK LESLIE JEFFCOAT. Ventura resident Jeffcoat enlisted in the Army in 1942 and became a glider pilot. When the war ended, he utilized the GI Bill and enrolled in courses at the University of Southern California, which eventually led him to a career with Northrup Grumman Corporation. (Courtesy of Shelly Foote.)

WALTER MORENO. Santa Paula resident Moreno served in the Army Air Corps from 1942 until the end of the war in 1946. He flew more than 25 successful missions over Germany. He continued to serve in the Air Force until 1954, retiring with the rank of major. (Courtesy of Al Perez.)

War Dog Platoon. In 1943, after receiving permission from his mother, Camarillo resident Bruce Wellington enlisted in the Marine Corps when he was only 17 years old. While training at Parris Island, South Carolina, Wellington was told about a new program called the "War Dog Platoon." He was sent to Camp LeJeune, North Carolina, to train with the 2nd War Dog Platoon, eventually pairing up with a six-year-old German shepherd named Prince. Prince remained Wellington's dog even after the war ended. (Courtesy Bruce Wellington.)

Orville Main. Camarillo resident Main was selected for pilot training in the Army Air Corps in 1942. In April 1944, he graduated from advanced training, specializing in B-17s. Main flew 35 missions over Germany from December 1944 through April 1945. He continued his service as an Air Force Reserve and went on to work as a pilot for American Airlines. (Courtesy of Carol Bachman.)

A WOMAN MARINE. On October 23, 1943, Camarillo resident Ruth Pettijohn enlisted in the Marines, but there was one hitch—she did not weigh enough. She was told she needed to gain six pounds before she could be sworn in. For that entire day, Pettijohn drank whole milk and ate bananas and graham crackers. By four that afternoon, Pettijohn met the weight requirement and was sworn in. She served stateside until October 1945. (Courtesy of Ruth Pettijohn.)

AN ADMIRAL'S INSPECTION. Adm. William Halsey inspects the USS *Ticonderoga* in the Pacific. The ship's photographer Thomas Ford took the photograph. A resident of Thousand Oaks, Ford captured important moments in the ship's history during the two years that the ship was active in World War II. (Courtesy of Thomas Ford.)

TONY MORUA. Santa Paula resident Morua served as a front line combat medic for the Army in the Philippines and throughout New Guinea and Japan. (Courtesy of Jay Widdows and Patti Morua-Widdows.)

COAST GUARD. Santa Paula resident Gil Asa, a member of the Coast Guard, served aboard the USS *Leonard Wood* delivering troops and supplies ashore in the Pacific. He also assisted in retrieving casualties from the front lines, bringing them back to the ship. Asa's landings included the Marshall and Gilbert Islands, Saipan, and Leyte. (Courtesy of Jay Widdows and Patti Morua-Widdows.)

USS THETIS BAY. Ventura resident Robert Tveit enlisted in the Navy and served aboard a landing ship tank through the invasion of Normandy, France. He was then transferred to the USS *Thetis Bay*, an aircraft carrier that took Tveit to battle in the Pacific. (Courtesy of Connie Tveit.)

COCKTAILS. Santa Paula resident Robert McKaig is pictured with his wife, Jeanne, at a Los Angeles restaurant in 1945. McKaig was an Army pilot and flew a C-47 cargo plane over the Himalaya Mountains from India to China. (Courtesy of Mike McKaig.)

RUTH CHRISTENSEN. Simi Valley resident Christensen enlisted in the Women's Army Corps in March 1943, along with her good friend Carol who talked Christensen in taking a chance at adventure. Christensen was sent overseas on active duty while Carol—who had wanted to go overseas—remained stateside. Christensen worked as a secretary in New Guinea and Manila until the end of the war. (Courtesy of Ruth Christensen.)

A VOLUNTEER'S SPIRIT. From the moment Santa Paula resident Roy Jennings was drafted into the Army, he decided he would volunteer for any task that was needed. This included carrying a 35-pound pack of explosive powder across enemy lines during the Battle of Metz, which was used to destroy an enemy bunker. It was a success. Jennings returned to California and taught history at Santa Paula High School for more than 30 years. (Courtesy of Mark Jennings.)

FRIENDS IN UNIFORM. Emery "Sam" Starkweather (left), who is pictured here with two friends, enlisted in the Navy on July 4, 1942. The Ojai resident served in the Pacific as a radioman aboard the USS *Rosewood* (YN-26), the USS *Indianapolis*, the USS *New Jersey*, and the USS *Hendry*. Starkweather witnessed the famous raising of the American flag on Iwo Jima, a memory he fondly recalls. (Courtesy of Emery "Sam" Starkweather.)

LOVE LETTERS. Much of Charles and Eleanor VanDelinder's courtship was through love letters. Charles enlisted in the National Guard in 1940. The Oxnard man served stateside until he was sent overseas as a gunner with the 41st Division. He participated in the D-Day invasion and fought through France and into Germany until the Germans surrendered in May 1945. (Courtesy of Charles and Eleanor VanDelinder.)

RALPH NOLL. Ventura resident Noll was drafted into the Army in June 1943 and was attached to the 832nd Anti-Aircraft Battalion. He trained as part of a 40-mm gun crew and was sent to fight in France where he was wounded when a grenade exploded near him. After the attack, he was taken as a POW by the Germans. He was not released until March 1945 and weighed only 89 pounds. (Courtesy of Steve Noll.)

PAUL BACKMAN. Ventura resident Backman enlisted in the Army after graduating from USC's dental program in 1942. He was attached to the 7th Infantry Division as a medic and aided his fellow comrades in battle in the Pacific, including in Leyte and Okinawa. (Courtesy of Jill Backman Hessick.)

A SEGREGATED ARMY. Oxnard resident Milton Graham was among approximately 1.2 million blacks who were either drafted or volunteered for military duty when segregation still plagued much of the country. He was assigned to a labor battalion and was separated from other soldiers. He fought through France and Germany but was initially overlooked for the medals he earned during his service. It was not until 1998 that Graham received his medals. (Courtesy of the Milton Graham family.)

MANUEL DE LOS SANTOS. Saticoy resident De Los Santos (right) sailed to Cherbourg, France, as a BAR man with the 104th Infantry Division on August 2, 1944. His first combat experience was in Belgium, and he continued to fight valiantly throughout Holland and Germany. He was wounded by a German sniper on April 1, 1945. De Los Santos was eventually discharged from the Army in November of that year. (Courtesy of Mike De Los Santos.)

NAVY ENSIGN. Santa Paula resident Richard Vincent enlisted in the Navy. Vincent served as an ensign and eventually as a lieutenant commander throughout the Pacific. One of his last active duty experiences included coming into Hiroshima after the atomic bomb had been dropped in 1945. He noted that the Japanese citizens welcomed him and his shipmates graciously, an act that stunned him. (Courtesy of Audrey Vincent.)

ROBERT CUNNINGHAM. Ventura resident Cunningham was inducted into the Army on May 11, 1942. He was activated the same day and was sent to Fort MacArthur, California, for basic training. He served with the 242nd Field Artillery Battalion in Northern France and Rhineland from July 13, 1944 to November 1945. He sailed home on the USS *LeJeune* on November 4, 1945. (Courtesy of Joe Jauregui.)

MIDWAY, 1944. This photograph of Rafael Jimenez, formerly of Santa Paula, was taken on Midway Island in late 1944. Jimenez arrived on Midway as a member of the Marine Corps in June 1943 and was assigned duties as a payroll clerk, earning $50 per month. (Courtesy of Rafael Jimenez.)

RAYMOND HARTWICK. Santa Paula resident Hartwick (second from right) served as an electrician's mate, first class, aboard the USS *Marcus Island* in the South Pacific. (Courtesy of Susan Hartwick-Sauer.)

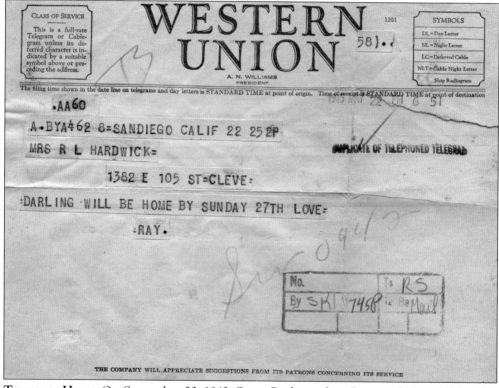

TELEGRAM HOME. On September 20, 1943, Santa Paula resident Raymond Hartwick left his home and his wife, Leona, in Ohio and headed to war. On May 22, 1945, at 6:51 p.m., he sent this Western Union telegram to Leona notifying her that he would soon be home. (Courtesy of Susan Hartwick-Sauer.)

PETE ROMERO. Santa Paula resident Romero fought as a squad leader with the 145th Infantry Regiment in New Guinea and the Philippines. He was active in the Army from March 19, 1943 to December 18, 1945. (Courtesy of Alice Romero.)

OTIS MOORE. Santa Paula resident Moore left the United States on September 19, 1944, and arrived in England on October 2, 1944. He fought through France with the 43rd Tank Battalion until January 16, 1945, when he was captured by the Germans and taken as a POW. He remained a prisoner for 102 days but was freed on April 29, 1945. (Courtesy of Kristi Viramontes.)

MARINE CORPS RESERVE. Newbury Park resident James Lieberknecht enlisted as a Marine Corps Reserve on July 5, 1940, which was a little more than a year before the bombing of Pearl Harbor. He was put on active duty in November of that year and began training as a radio operator. He served 32 months in the Pacific, including on the Solomon Islands of Tulagi and Guadalcanal, as well as on Saipan, Guam, and Iwo Jima. (Courtesy of James Lieberknecht.)

1944 HILO, HAWAII

FLIGHT OFFICER. Pictured is Camarillo resident Jack Templin in the freight office at Tempelhof Airport in Berlin, Germany, in 1945. Templin served as a flight officer and glider pilot in Europe. (Courtesy Jack Templin.)

VENTURA FRIENDS. Ventura resident Harvey Kellog (left) poses with his friend David Drapeau, also a Venturan, in Missouri before being sent overseas. (Courtesy of Beverly Drapeau.)

JACK LARIMORE. Ventura resident Larimore is pictured in front of one of the trucks he drove for the Marine Corps. During his service, Larimore worked as a supply truck and ambulance driver. (Courtesy of Mary Ellen Ledbetter.)

JOHN "BUD" GOODING. Santa Paula resident Gooding served in the Army during the infamous Battle of the Bulge in the winter of 1944 through 1945. Gooding was initially assigned as a rifleman with the 101st Airborne Division. After several weeks of fighting, Gooding took the demolition skills he learned and put them to use against the Germans. (Courtesy of John "Bud" Gooding.)

HOLOCAUST SURVIVOR. In 1938, Ventura resident Bernd Simon was just 18 years old when the Gestapo burst into his home. They took him and his mother as prisoners to Dachau, which was a concentration camp near Munich. In 1940, Simon fled the camp and headed to Cuba, where he boarded a ship bound for New York. He enlisted in the Army and became a US citizen, which enabled him to fight the Germans throughout Europe. (Courtesy of Bernd Simon.)

PEARL HARBOR SURVIVOR. Ventura resident Walter Furst was stationed at Pearl Harbor when the Japanese attacked on December 7, 1941. When the attack began, Seaman Furst thought that the Army might be holding target practice. However, he said, it soon became apparent that it was not the case. (Courtesy of Walter Furst.)

RANCHER SENT TO WAR. Daniel Robert "Bob" Jauregui, who was 23 years old, was living on the family ranch in Santa Paula when he enlisted in the Army Air Corps in 1941. He served as a first lieutenant bombardier aboard a B-24, flying more than 48 missions in the Philippines and South Pacific. (Courtesy of Shirley Jauregui.)

WILLIAM LUCKING JR. Ojai resident Lucking Jr. enlisted as a Navy Reserve in 1940, serving as a skipper on coastal defense operations. When the war began, he was stationed aboard the USS *Prichett* as an executive officer. Here, he is pictured with his wife, Helen, in 1944. (Courtesy Helen Fredell.)

RALPH WILSON HAUGHT. Ventura resident Haught began his time in the Army on January 5, 1942. He fought through France, serving as a sergeant to his platoon before being promoted to staff sergeant with the 1001th Engineering Forestry Battalion. (Courtesy of Penny Allen.)

A Colonel. Santa Paula resident Tom Rafferty was a paratrooper who eventually served as a colonel in the Army. He was attached to the 71st Division in France and Germany, and he became the recipient of two Silver Star medals, two Bronze Star medals, and a Purple Heart. (Courtesy Lois Rafferty.)

Albaro "Bob" Chavez Macias. Santa Paula resident Macias was a marine aircraft mechanic in the Pacific from 1942 through 1946. (Courtesy of Ana Maria Lopez.)

AVIATION MECHANIC. Santa Paula resident William "Bill" Florio was assigned duties as an aviation mechanic in the Marine Corps. It was a short stint as he was soon reassigned duties as a gunner. He also received radar training. Soon after, he found himself flying missions in Manila, Corregidor Island, and Bataan. (Courtesy William "Bill" Florio.)

WILLIAM McCLARD. In 1944, Camarillo resident McClard fought with the 84th Division, 309th Engineer Combat Battalion, Company C in the Battle of the Bulge in Belgium. Prior to that, he had served actively in France and went on to serve in Germany until the war ended in May 1945. (Courtesy of Amanda McClard.)

A COLONEL'S ROOTS. The first military uniform that Ralph "Bud" Vandervort wore was an Army uniform from World War I as a requirement for his ROTC program. In 1941, Camarillo resident Vandervort was commissioned as a second lieutenant and received a uniform of his own. He fought in Europe and continued his service through 1961, retiring as a colonel. He went on to serve as a congressional liaison and then as associate director of the Peace Corps. (Courtesy of Ralph "Bud" Vandervort family.)

ALVIN MEISSNER. Ventura resident Meissner (right) was drafted into the Army in 1942, serving with the 362nd Infantry Regiment in Italy. Taken in June 1944, he is pictured in Naples, Italy, with a Native American serviceman identified as "Chief" with whom he became friends. (Courtesy of Jessie McLeod.)

MARINE AVIATION. Oxnard resident Allen Gilbert, a marine radio operator aboard a B-25, served in the air during the invasion of Okinawa in March 1945. He wanted to experience ground combat and went on the island only to come face-to-face with the enemy. Gilbert saved the life of a wounded Japanese man with whom he became friends by the end of the war. (Courtesy of Allen Gilbert.)

WEDDING BELLS. Oxnard resident Bud Snyder enlisted in the Navy on January 7, 1942. He was stationed aboard the USS *Bogue* and USS *Hornet* during World War II. He decided to have a military career and continued to serve on the USS *Block Island*, USS *Mindoro*, USS *Princeton*, and USS *Hancock* until he retired on July 9, 1961. Here, Snyder is pictured on his wedding day on July 1, 1946, with his wife, Virginia, whom he fondly refers to as "G." (Courtesy of Bud Snyder.)

WAR AND A NEW LANGUAGE. In January 1943, Santa Paula resident Albino Pineda volunteered for active duty in the Army, a decision he made even though he knew very little English. While training on 155-mm guns, Pineda was studying English on the side and quickly became fluent. He was eventually sent to combat in Europe in August 1944, and he was attached to the 9th Army Division. (Courtesy Albino Pineda.)

LOVE BLOOMS IN WAR. Wayne Downing enlisted in the Army Air Corps in the summer of 1941 after finishing his third year of college at the University of Denver. While training in England, he heard about a dance hosted by American Army nurses. He went and met Norma, a nurse with the 298th General Hospital. This photograph was taken in England on one of the couple's dates. They were married soon after. (Courtesy Wayne and Norma Downing, Thousand Oaks.)

ARMY PILOT. Santa Paula resident Robert Grainger enlisted in the Army Air Corps in February 1943, and soon after began training in the aviation cadet program. He earned his wings in May 1944. Here, Grainger is pictured beside the nose of a P-38 Lightning while stationed in Japan. He continued his service through Vietnam and retired with the rank of major. (Courtesy of Robert Grainger.)

ROBERT HERRON. The Hollywood stuntman was drafted into the Navy straight out of high school. He was sent to sonar training and eventually shipped out to Pearl Harbor. Herron, a resident of Thousand Oaks, was then shipped to the Marshall Islands to prepare for the invasion of Saipan in the summer of 1942. He continued his service through the Pacific, including patrols around the Philippines and the Solomon Islands, as well as the invasion of Okinawa. (Courtesy of Robert Herron.)

FLYING TIGERS. Oxnard resident John Ramirez was one of three sons of Celsa and Manuel Ramirez that was sent to World War II. He volunteered for duty in the Army Air Corps on June 27, 1942. He was assigned to the 23rd Fighter Group that was more commonly known as the "Flying Tigers," and he flew missions in India and China. (Courtesy of John Ramirez.)

JIM WHITE. Ventura resident White (left) was drafted into the Navy in 1943 and served aboard the USS *Gasconade* as a radar operator. He was discharged in 1946, but he served seven years in the Navy Reserves This photograph was taken with a Japanese friend in Nagoya, Japan, in November 1945. (Courtesy of Jim White.)

A COMBAT POSE. Joe Martinez is pictured in uniform. (Courtesy of Joe Martinez family.)

GENE YPARRAGUIRRE. Oxnard resident Yparraguirre's war story begins on December 8, 1941, one day after Pearl Harbor was bombed. The 19-year-old Gene went to the enlistment office in Ventura to join the Navy with his brother Joe. The two were sworn in on December 30, 1941, and they boarded a bus bound for boot camp at the Naval Base in San Diego. During his time in the Navy, Yparraguirre was stationed aboard the USS *Saratoga* in the Pacific and participated in battles in New Guinea and the invasion of Bougainville Island. (Courtesy of Gene Yparraguirre.)

PARATROOPER. Oxnard resident John D. Figueroa, an Army paratrooper, jumped into Holland to help liberate the country on September 17, 1944. He was wounded on October 5, 1944. He spent the next two years in hospitals stateside. Figueroa (middle) poses with two of his therapists. (Courtesy of John D. Figueroa.)

BATAAN DEATH MARCH. In early April 1942, Ventura resident John Real was among the American and Filipino troops in a treacherous and losing battle against the Japanese in Bataan. Within days a decision was made. The American and Filipino forces would have to surrender. Real, who was with an observation squad with the Army Air Corps, had been fighting from a mountaintop. When the surrender became official, he made the eight-mile walk down the mountain to an unknown fate—one he knew may end with him dead. After walking down the mountain, the prisoners began the Bataan Death March, which was an approximate 60-mile walk to San Fernando. Real recalled, "Anyone that fell out of formation was killed instantly. It seemed that no matter how fast I tried to walk, I was always at the end of the line. But once I'd see a guy get killed, it sped me up." Real survived the Bataan Death March. This photograph was taken by the Japanese while Real was their prisoner. (Courtesy of John Real.)

Two

THE KOREAN WAR

A PROUD MOMENT.
Ventura resident Art
Karma receives the
Distinguished Flying
Cross on July 11, 1953,
by his group commander.
He served a total of 21
years in the Air Force,
retiring as a lieutenant
colonel in 1972.
(Courtesy of Art Karma.)

JuLy 1953   D.F.C.

HERBERT HUTCHINSON. The Westlake Village resident poses with a Korean orphan in Yong Dong Po, South Korea, in July 1953. He had been on active duty with the Army Corps of Engineers in South Korea. Hutchinson was a combat engineer platoon leader with the 8th Army Coalition, supporting the United Nations peacekeeping team. (Courtesy of Herbert Hutchinson.)

SURGICAL NURSE, 1953. Westlake Village resident Arline Hutchinson was a surgical nurse for the Navy, serving at the US Naval Hospital in St. Albans, New York. (Courtesy of Herbert Hutchinson.)

ROBERT RICHARDSON. Frazier Park resident Richardson was in the Air Force from 1955 to 1959. He served as a radar approach controller at March Air Force Base in Riverside, California, and Mather Air Force Base in Sacramento. (Courtesy of Robert Richardson.)

MILITARY POLICE. Henry Guevara served with the 505th Military Police Battalion at the Atomic Bomb Test Center in Camp Desert Rock, Nevada. (Courtesy of Henry Guevara.)

CALVIN D. DEETER. When the Korean War began, the 40th Infantry Division was the first National Guard unit to be activated. On November 1, 1950, the troops gathered in Santa Paula for the train trip to Camp Cook, which is now Vandenberg Air Force Base. Sfc. Calvin D. Deeter (left) trained with the 40th Infantry Division but was sent as a replacement to the 25th Infantry Division, which was already serving in Korea. Originally from Fillmore, Deeter was wounded while he was with the artillery group that was serving just north of the 38th parallel. He was sent to Osaka, Japan, for surgery on his leg and was awarded the Purple Heart on March 20, 1952. He returned to Camp Stoneman and was discharged on May 27, 1952. (Courtesy of Calvin D. Deeter.)

JOHN ADAMS FORD.
Ventura resident Ford was a sergeant at his unit's home base at Yong Dong Po, South Korea. In a biography, Ford described a New Year's Eve spent at Yong Dong Po, and he said, "I went outside to gas up the generator, when all the guns at the front opened up, . . . the whole northern sky lit up like the Fourth of July. I assumed we were telling the North Koreans, 'Happy New Year.'" (Courtesy of Glenna Fewell.)

FERNANDO MARTINEZ. Santa Paula resident Martinez was inducted into the Army on September 1, 1950, when he was just 16 years old. He served nearly two years and was discharged on July 31, 1952. (Courtesy of Helen Martinez.)

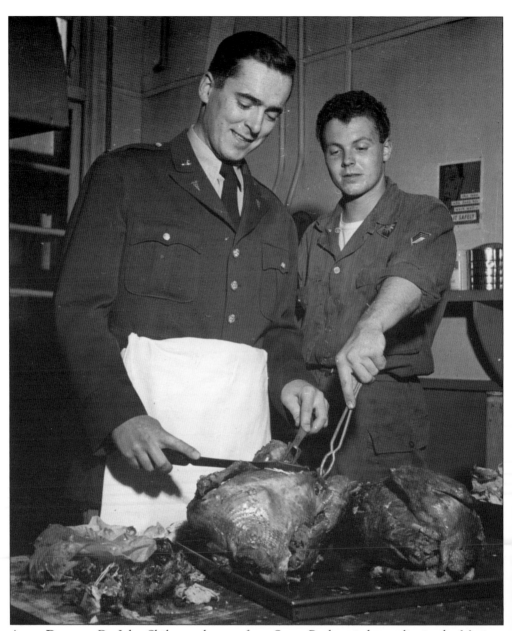

Army Doctor. Dr. John Shilton, who was from Santa Paula, tried to enlist in the Marines after Pearl Harbor was bombed in December 1941, but he received a medical rejection due to his eyesight. The marine surgeon conducting his exam thought Shilton would be a good marine. The surgeon gave Shilton a copy of the eye exam to study and retake the next day. Shilton's father, however, thought the tactic to be unethical. Instead, Shilton was drafted into the Army in 1942 and served stateside, eventually deciding to join the Army Medical Corps. From 1946 to 1949, he attended USC's Keck School of Medicine. During his second year of residency in 1950, he was called into the Doctor's Draft for the Korean War. This photograph was taken on Thanksgiving in 1951, after Shilton was chosen to carve the turkey. He served 16 months as a doctor and surgeon overseas. Afterwards, Shilton continued his medical services in Santa Paula. (Courtesy of Carol Jean Shilton.)

MANUEL MENDEZ. This Santa Paula resident was drafted into the Army in 1951. He served on active duty in Germany until the war ended in 1953. (Courtesy of Manuel Mendez Jr.)

ED SCHULTZ. The Ventura resident served as a private first class in the Army from 1951 to 1953. He worked in a machine records unit. Schultz also served as in the Navy Reserve from 1947 to 1951. (Courtesy of Ed Schultz.)

PEACETIME SERVICE. Ventura resident Darryl Struth served in the Navy between wars. In 1955, he was a painter aboard the USS *Kearsarge* when this photograph was taken with a fellow shipmate. His time in the Navy ended in 1959, which was only a few years before the United States would send the first group of troops to Vietnam. (Courtesy of Darryl Struth.)

SERVICE CONTINUED. Having served in World War II, Rafael Jimenez's second time serving during wartime was in the Korean War. Originally from Santa Paula, Jimenez was called to active duty once again on July 21, 1950, and initially remained stateside on recruiting duty in Fresno and San Francisco. He went on to serve in Guam and the Mariana Islands but eventually returned to California at the end of the war. (Courtesy of Rafael Jimenez.)

JOE LIMON. Santa Paula resident Limon was stationed in South Korea after he was inducted into the Army on January 1, 1950. He was a member of a construction battalion until he was discharged on September 18, 1952. (Courtesy of Frances Limon.)

BLU ON THE BOTTOM PI '51

HAVING A LAUGH. Simi Valley resident Mort Zwicker stands on a friend's shoulder behind a 13th Air Force sign in 1951. (Courtesy of Mort Zwicker.)

NAVY CORPSMAN. Santa Paula resident Delton Lee Johnson served as a corpsman with the Navy, where he cared for the wounded and sick troops in Korea. He was put on active duty in February 1951 and was discharged in February 1955. (Courtesy of Delton Lee Johnson.)

JESS AGUIRRE. Santa Paula resident Aguirre was drafted into the Army in 1950. He was assigned duties with the 4th Infantry Division. He was supposed to be sent to Korea, but when a fellow soldier went "absent without official leave," or AWOL in the military, Aguirre was called into the sergeant's office. He was told that he would take that soldier's place in Germany, which was a decision that likely saved his life. (Courtesy of Mark Aguirre.)

STATIONED IN GERMANY. Port Hueneme resident Peter Cavallo poses in front of an Army vehicle in May 1953 in Hanover, Germany. Cavallo served in the Army from 1951 to 1953. (Courtesy of Peter Cavallo.)

"BORROWED" SIGN. Michael Loftus poses in front of a Ventura city limit sign that was borrowed from home. He served in the Army from September 1, 1950 to May 8, 1952. Prior to the Korean War, Loftus served in the National Guard and was stationed in Japan. (Courtesy of Michael Loftus.)

RAYMOND PRICE. Newbury Park resident Price (left) stands in a gun pit that was on top of a mountain and just south of the Punch Bowl in South Korea. His duty was to guard the area with a 50-caliber machine gun as a member of the 45th Infantry Division. (Courtesy of Raymond Price.)

BOOT CAMP. Ventura resident George Rose poses for a 1951 photograph at boot camp in San Diego. He served as an electrician's mate in the Navy from January 1951 to December 1954. He completed tours to Alaska, Japan, and the Marshall Islands. (Courtesy of George Rose.)

RADIO OPERATOR. In December 1950, Santa Paula resident Hector Borrego was drafted into the Army. Soon after, he was selected to become a radio operator for the 35th Infantry Regiment in the 25th Infantry Division. He served in South Korea and was discharged from the Army on October 3, 1952. (Courtesy of Connie Borrego.)

DONALD SEVERS. Newbury Park resident Severs served aboard the USS *Kearsarge* during the evacuation of the Tachen Islands. He was active in the Navy from 1951 to 1955. Severs poses here with a nice background view of Japan. (Courtesy of Gloria Severs.)

B-36 Crew Chief. Ventura resident Dean Jernigan served as a crew chief in charge of maintenance aboard a B-36. The "Peacemaker," as the plane was called, could fly at an altitude of 45,700 feet, could go 10,000 miles without refueling, and travel at 435 miles per hour. Jernigan enlisted in the Air Force on October 16, 1949, and was discharged on October 17, 1953. (Courtesy of Dean Jernigan.)

Eutimeo Beas. Oxnard resident Beas smiles for a quick photograph while stationed at Fort Knox, Kentucky, as a member of an Army tank battalion. (Courtesy of Rachel Beas.)

Henry Bellew. Santa Paula resident Bellew enlisted in the Air Force in 1947 and served in Guam until November 1950, which is when he was sent on active duty to Korea. He remained in Korea until January 1951 as a member of the 934th Signal Battalion, supplying the communications network for the Fifth Air Force. (Courtesy of Shirley Bellew.)

Kenneth O'Connell. Oxnard resident O'Connell enlisted in the California National Guard in August 1949. When the war began, he was attached to the 40th Infantry Division and was sent to Camp Cook, which is now Vandenberg Air Force Base. The only problem was that the base had been shut down after World War II. The troops had to start from scratch, only to pack everything up within six months when they shipped out to Japan. (Courtesy of Kenneth O'Connell.)

OCTOBER 25, 1953

CALIFORNIANS MEET—During his recent visit to the 40th Infantry Division in Korea, Congressman Robert C. Wilson (R-Calif) stopped to talk with Division men from California. Pvt. Jose A. Ramirze, Company F, 223rd Infantry Regiment, from Carnarillo, Calif., talks over the affairs of their home state with the congressman. To the right of Ramirze is Pvt. Louis Lugo, Company H, 223rd Regiment, Santa Barbara, California.

CONGRESSIONAL VISIT. Camarillo resident Jose Ramirez is photographed in a South Korean newspaper when he met with Robert Wilson, congressman from California, who was visiting the war-torn country. Ramirez was drafted into the Army in 1952 and served with the 40th Infantry Division, which was a National Guard Unit. (Courtesy of Jose Ramirez.)

DAVID CLAPPERTON. Santa Paula resident Clapperton enlisted in the Navy on June 28, 1948. Clapperton served through much of the Korean War until he was discharged on June 27, 1952. He trained at the Naval Aeronautical Technical Training Center in Memphis before he was transferred to the Miramar Naval Air Station, where he worked in the metal shop. He also worked in the metal shop while serving aboard the USS *Boxer* in 1950. (Courtesy of David Clapperton.)

Three

THE VIETNAM WAR

MY FAMILIA. Sgt. Reynaldo Frutos, who is pictured holding two children, said it best. Recalling his experiences on the war, Santa Paula resident Frutos said, "Whenever we came to a village, I always seemed to get attached to the kids. I personally come from a rather large family, and I missed my brothers and sisters. I would connect with the children, and they became my familia. Now that I look back, the children are what made me feel better about being in Vietnam. They really made you forget about the war, even if it was only for a few hours." (Courtesy of Reynaldo Frutos.)

CHRISTMAS IN VIETNAM. Santa Paula resident Reynaldo Frutos served in Vietnam from April 10, 1970 to May 4, 1971. Here, he is pictured with his Christmas tree in December 1970. He said, "It wasn't a white Christmas, but it was a dusty one." (Courtesy of Reynaldo Frutos.)

ENGINE ROOM. Ventura resident Thomas Cirricione poses in the engine room of a ship he was working on while stationed in Bremerton, Washington. Cirricione served as a petty officer from 1962 to 1969, completing two tours in North Vietnam. (Courtesy of Thomas Cirricione.)

JOHNNY HURTADO. Fillmore resident Hurtado poses while on active duty on October 10, 1971. (Courtesy of Johnny Hurtado.)

BILL BURATTO. Thousand Oaks resident Buratto served as a medical laboratory technician for the 91st EVAC Hospital in Chu Lai, Vietnam, from 1970 to 1971. The lab was made up of two interconnected Quonset huts that were broken up into sections for a blood bank, hematology, chemistry, and bacteriology. Here, Buratto (foreground) is pictured with friend and comrade Jim "Buzz" Galvin. (Courtesy of Bill Buratto.)

A Seabee. In 1966, Santa Paula resident Charlie Stine was called to active duty overseas as part of a Seabee construction battalion. His tour included duties in Da Nang, Vietnam; Cambodia; and the Philippines. Taken in 1967, this photograph shows Stine while he was stationed in Da Nang. (Courtesy of Candice Jones.)

Dennis Behrens. Former Santa Paula resident Behrens began his military career during the Vietnam War and continued to serve until he eventually earned the rank of colonel. (Courtesy of Clara Behrens.)

JERRY HOLLADAY. Ventura resident Holladay enlisted in the Army when he was 19 years old, and he joined to do his part in the war effort. He was stationed in Hanau, Germany, from 1964 to 1967, working as a supply clerk who picked up and delivered equipment when needed. (Courtesy of Jerry Holladay.)

STATESIDE SERVICE. Santa Paula resident James Cavender received his draft notice in 1965, but he decided to enlist in the Marine Corps Reserve based out of Port Hueneme. In just under a year, he was discharged from active duty. He served five and a half years as an active reserve, training throughout Southern California. Taken in 1969, this photograph shows Cavender holding an M60 machine gun during amphibious landing training on Coronado Island, San Diego. (Courtesy of James Cavender.)

BEST FRIENDS. Darrel Bice (left) and Terry Powers (right) were best friends at Ventura High School, graduating just one year apart from one another. They were both marines and served overseas together for a period of time. Here, the pair is pictured during Christmas in Okinawa, Japan, in 1967. Only a few months later, they were both promoted to the rank of sergeant. (Courtesy of Terry Powers.)

RODOLFO SANTIAGO. Simi Valley resident Santiago is pictured in the berthing compartment of the USS *Somers.* The ship had been on patrol off the coast of Vietnam, providing support for the troops stationed on shore. Santiago served in the Navy from May 1967 to May 1971, and he continued his service beyond the war as a Navy Reserve. (Courtesy of Rodolfo Santiago.)

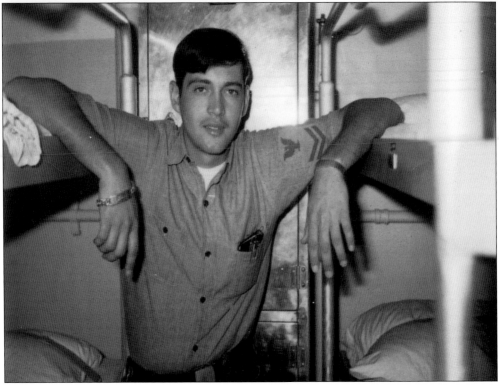

HIS THIRD WAR. Rafael Jimenez received orders to report for active duty in June 1964 and was sent to combat in Vietnam. It was his third war. However, when he arrived, Jimenez was sent to Guam for treatment because of a stomach condition, which allowed him to serve his tour in Japan instead. After 20 years of service, he retired from the Marines on December 31, 1966. (Courtesy of Rafael Jimenez.)

DAVE BETTI. Oak View resident Betti was drafted into the Army in 1969. While at the induction center, Betti decided he wanted to enlist in the Marine Corps to pay homage to his father and grandfather. He was assigned to the 1st Battalion, 7th Marines Regiment, 1st Marine Division, and he was in combat in Vietnam from June 1970 to June 1971. Here, he is pictured with his mother, Ruth, and his sister Lynn. (Courtesy of Dave Betti.)

A NOTE TO LINDA. Santa Paula resident Frank Fierroz signed the back of this Navy portrait with a note to his future wife, Linda. In part it read, "Here's a picture of me so you won't forget me while I'm far away from you. Don't ever forget that I love you always." Fierroz served tours in Vietnam, Japan, and China aboard the USS *Samuel Gompers*. (Courtesy of Linda Fierroz.)

DON TURNER, 1970. Oxnard resident Turner served as a Seabee from October 1954 to August 1995. In this photograph, Turner (right) prepares to take a flight over a small airfield in Vietnam that needed repairs. (Courtesy of Don Turner.)

HIGH SCHOOL SWEETHEARTS. Jerry Norton, formerly from Santa Paula, is pictured with his wife, Carole, on their wedding day in January 22, 1966, at the First Presbyterian Church in Santa Paula. The couple graduated from high school together in 1965. Norton enlisted in the Air Force in August 1965 and served at Elmendorf Air Force Base in Anchorage, Alaska, from December 1965 to February 1969. (Courtesy of Jerry Norton.)

PHOTOGRAPH WITH A HERO. Westlake Village resident James Ziegler (left) is pictured with a man who saved his life during the Tet Offensive in 1968. Ziegler served as an intelligence specialist in the Army in Vietnam from September 1967 to July 1968. (Courtesy of James Ziegler.)

Jim Edison. Ventura resident Edison (left) arrived in Vietnam in March 1969, and he was assigned to the 5th Special Forces Group in Nha Trang. Soon after, he was reassigned to the 5th Mike Force. The diet included dehydrated rice with a flavor packet, which was usually beef or shrimp. In order to make their rice and heat the water mixed in it, they had to tear off a chunk of C-4, an explosive device, and ignite it with a lighter. (Courtesy of Jim Edison.)

Carlos Magdaleno. Santa Paula resident Magdaleno poses in front of a tank that he was completing maintenance work on. Magdaleno was part of the Army's 2nd Maintenance Battalion in Vung Tau, Vietnam. (Courtesy of Carlos Magdaleno.)

BRUCE CAMPBELL. Former Santa Paula resident Campbell graduated from the Naval Training Center in San Diego on October 2, 1964. He was sent to Data Processing Technician A-School, and soon after, he received orders to board the USS *Bryce Canyon*. As a data processing technician, Campbell performed various data-entry duties, including payroll and inventory, during the ship's tours to Pearl Harbor, Japan, Taiwan, and the Philippines. (Courtesy of Bruce Campbell.)

A YOUNG AIRMAN. In 1962, Ventura resident Ron Rosenow enlisted in the Air Force when he was 17 years old, which started his nearly 12-year stint as an airman. Rosenow, who is standing second from left, is photographed with his crew from the 553rd Reconnaissance Squadron at Korat Air Base in Thailand. Their mission was to fly over Hanoi to collect intelligence about the location of the Viet Cong. (Courtesy of Ron Rosenow.)

HIGH SCHOOL BUDDIES. Taken in 1968, Warren "Butch" Handrock (right) and John Hartshorn (left), classmates from Santa Paula High School, pose for a photograph in Vietnam. (Courtesy of Warren "Butch" Handrock.)

ALFREDO VERA. Santa Paula resident Vera, who was in the Army, is pictured at his home base in Cu Chi, Vietnam. (Courtesy of Olga Vera.)

PROMOTION. Santa Paula resident Frank Guzman poses in May 1967 as he is promoted to sergeant at the duty station in Furth, Germany. Guzman was a member of a tactical data unit with the Seventh Army. (Courtesy of Frank Guzman.)

ARMY CAREER. Santa Paula resident Gerald Olivas enlisted in the Army in August 1960, just weeks after he graduated from high school. He trained with heavy weapons and antitank weapons, including the 105 Recoilless Rifle and the SS-10 antitank missile. He was first sent to serve in Korea. He then completed tours in Germany, Japan, and South Vietnam. After 20 years of service, Olivas retired from the Army in 1980. (Courtesy of Gerald Olivas.)

JIM ABING. Ventura resident Abing, who was a recent civil engineering graduate, volunteered to serve as a Seabee in 1960. He served two deployments to Okinawa, one to Guam, and a final tour in Vietnam, working on construction jobs, including roads, bridges, and air strips, in the highlands of South Vietnam. (Courtesy Jim Abing.)

A Soldier Returns. Santa Paula resident Peter Aguirre is welcomed home with this newspaper clipping that declared his service in Vietnam with the 41st Infantry Battalion. (Courtesy of Mark Aguirre.)

RETURNS

JUST RETURNED after a year in Vietnam, Santa Paula soldier Peter Aguirre has been assigned to Fort Riley, Kans., to finish his military service. He took basic training at Fort Bliss, Texas, and while in Vietnam was with the 41st Infantry Battalion. A sergeant, he was married to the former Marie Martinez just prior to going to Vietnam. His parents are Mr. and Mrs. Don H. Aguirre.

John Arias. From January 1968 to January 1969, Oxnard resident Arias served in the Army while in Vietnam with the Delta Company, 1st of the 20th, 11th Light Infantry Brigade Americal Division. (Courtesy of John Arias.)

A NAVY CORPSMAN. Alan Jackson is pictured caring for an infant who was from a native tribe in the highlands of South Korea. According to comrade Jim Abing, Jackson was dedicated to his job, serving the people of the region day and night. (Courtesy of Jim Abing.)

BACK FROM FIRST OPERATION. Mike Bailey, formerly from Santa Paula, is pictured upon returning from his first operation in the field in 1967. He volunteered for the draft in 1966 and was assigned to the 1st Infantry Division. Bailey participated in several major operations, including Junction City in the Iron Triangle. (Courtesy of Mike Bailey.)

BRUCE ALAN LOCKHART. Santa Paula resident Lockhart is shown posing for a quick snapshot at the Nha Trang Air Base in South Vietnam in 1968. Lockhart served as a sergeant in the Air Force with the 20th Special Operations Squadron. (Courtesy of Bruce Alan Lockhart.)

LUCKY 32. Gregory Pale was number 32 in the draft lottery. He decided to enlist in the Army in March 1971, which was one month before his draft notice arrived at his home in Ventura. He served in the central highlands of South Vietnam as a member of the 344th Aviation Detachment Division. (Courtesy of Gregory Pale.)

DOUG THIEL. Ojai resident Thiel poses for a photograph in Da Nang, Vietnam, in December 1968. Thiel enlisted in the Marine Corps two years earlier, and he served stateside until 1968 when he volunteered for duty in Vietnam, which was after his brother was killed in training with the 101st Airborne Division. Most of his tour was spent with the 1st Marine Aircraft Wing. (Courtesy of Doug Thiel.)

Four

GENERATIONS SENT TO WAR

FOUR MARINES, ONE FAMILY.
The Contreras family from
Ojai sent four sons to the
Marines in Vietnam. Julio,
Charles, John, and David all
served from 1964 to 1969.
John was the only one who
never made it home. He
was killed in combat in Khe
Sahn in 1968 when he was
only 18 years old. Here, the
family poses for a picture
at a Marines recruitment
office. Pictured from left
to right are (first row)
Victor Contreras and David
Contreras; (second row) Cpl.
Julio Contreras, Pvt. John
Contreras, their mother
Esperanza, and L.Cpl. Charles
Contreras. David joined the
Marines two months after
this photograph was taken.
(Courtesy of Julio Contreras.)

CHARLES CONTRERAS. Julio Contreras described his brother Charles as an amazing athlete and magnificent marine. Charles had planned to make a career out of his service. However, shortly after returning from Vietnam, where he served with the 1st Marine Air Wing, Charles was killed by a drunk driver in an automobile accident. (Courtesy of Julio Contreras.)

JULIO CONTRERAS. Ojai resident Contreras trained at Camp Pendleton and in the Philippines before being sent to combat in Vietnam. (Courtesy of Julio Contreras.)

WALDO SISSON. Simi Valley resident Sisson enlisted in the Navy in 1943, which was just before his 18th birthday. He took a job that few others were interested in, operating and running projectors to show movies to his shipmates while at sea. Here, Sisson (left) is working with the film reel and the projector. (Courtesy of Vincent Nowell.)

VINCENT NOWELL. Taken in July 1959, Simi Valley resident Nowell is shown with his 1951 Mercury Sedan at Holloman Air Force Base, New Mexico. Nowell, who is a brother of Waldo Sisson, served in the Air Force from 1956 through 1960. (Courtesy of Vincent Nowell.)

TONY VASQUEZ SR. Santa Paula resident Vasquez Sr. served with the 30th Infantry Division throughout Europe until he was taken as a POW by the Germans on October 6, 1944. He escaped from the prison camp in January 1945 but was shot in the arm. He managed to make it out alive. Here, Vasquez (middle) is pictured with two friends while recovering at a stateside Army hospital. (Courtesy of Estella Cabral Arguelles.)

TONY VASQUEZ JR. Pictured here is the son of Tony Vasquez Sr. The Santa Paula resident served in the Army during the Vietnam War. (Courtesy of Tony Vasquez Jr.)

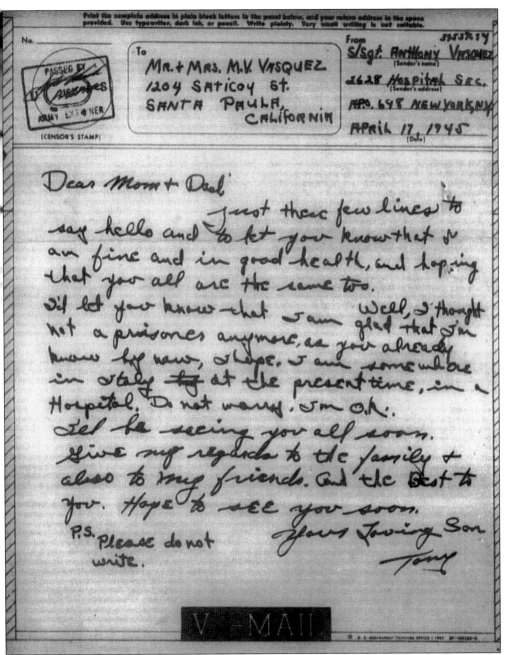

MARTIN VASQUEZ. The former Santa Paula resident served in the Marines from 1945 to 1975. He was in combat in Korea. Like his nephew Tony Vasquez Jr., he served a period of time in Vietnam as well. (Courtesy Martin Vasquez.)

FRANK VASQUEZ. Former Santa Paula resident Vasquez followed the footsteps of his brother Tony Vasquez Sr. and served in the Army from 1948 to 1952. He was first deployed to Japan, but he was later called to active duty when the Korean War began. (Courtesy of Martin Vasquez.)

WALTER ARTHUR BUNDE. Camarillo resident Bunde served in the Army from 1946 to 1948. He was stationed at Fort Gulick, Panama, where he became the baker and cook for his comrades. He used his helmet to measure ingredients, because measuring cups were not available. (Courtesy of Patricia Lincoln.)

MICHAEL WALTER BUNDE. Pictured here is the son of Walter Arthur Bunde, who followed his father into the Army, serving from 1968 to 1972. He was assigned to active duty in Germany. (Courtesy of Patricia Lincoln.)

JERRY SERROS. Oxnard resident Serros is pictured at Dhahran Air Force Base in Saudi Arabia in 1953. (Courtesy of Jerry Serros.)

ROBERT SERROS. Pictured here is Jerry Serros's brother Robert, who served in the Army's 1st Division in Germany in 1953. (Courtesy of Jerry Serros.)

MANUEL SERROS. Pictured here is Oxnard resident Manuel Serros, who was the uncle to Jerry and Robert. He served in Burma as a member of the Army during World War II. (Courtesy of Jerry Serros.)

JESSE DAVISON. Former Santa Paula resident Davison enlisted in the Marine Corps on December 11, 1942, and served through the end of the war in 1945. He was in combat in the Pacific and participated in operations on the Marshall Islands, Mariana Islands, and Iwo Jima. (Courtesy of Kay Davison-Culpepper and Nadine Ford.)

RALPH DAVISON. Picture here is the brother of Jesse Davison. Ralph worked in communications as a member of the National Guard, and he was in combat in Normandy, France, on D-Day in June 1944. Ralph also fought through the Battle of the Bulge in the winter of 1944. (Courtesy of Kay Davison-Culpepper and Nadine Ford.)

LINDEL DAVISON. Santa Paula resident Lindel, who was one of the Davison brothers, was a gunner for the Army. He was inducted on October 21, 1941, in Los Angeles and served in the Pacific until 1945. (Courtesy of Kay Davison-Culpepper and Nadine Ford.)

DEAN DAVISON. Dean Davison was the brother of Ralph, Lindel, and William. He served in the Army from December 14, 1943, to September 15, 1945. He was a member of the Transportation Corps in Europe, driving various vehicles and maintaining trip reports and mileage logs. (Courtesy of Kay Davison-Culpepper.)

WILLIAM DAVISON. Following in his four brothers' footsteps of military service, William was as an Army sergeant from 1950 to 1952. (Courtesy of Kay Davison-Culpepper.)

ARTHUR HERNANDEZ. Santa Paula resident Hernandez enlisted in the Navy on November 13, 1942, and he served in the Pacific, including Okinawa, until he was discharged on March 30, 1946. (Courtesy of Lisa Hernandez.)

JAMES HERNANDEZ. Pictured here is the son of Arthur Hernandez who was on his way to guard duty in Pleiku when this photograph was taken. James, also a resident of Santa Paula, enlisted in the Army in March 1969. He was a communications center specialist for the 21st Signal Group, 1st Signal Brigade, in Pleiku, Vietnam. He also served tours in Germany and Korea. (Courtesy of Lisa Hernandez.)

CHARLES McCONICA. Ventura resident McConica served in the Navy during World War II. Here, he is pictured in his formal Navy portrait. (Courtesy of Rosena McConica.)

BROTHERS REUNITE. In 1945, John McConica (left) and Charles McConica (right) reunite in Hawaii after months without seeing one another. John served in Army while Charles was a member of the Navy. The brothers were both preparing for the invasion of Japan. However, the war was over after the atomic bombs were dropped over Hiroshima and Nagasaki—an event that may have saved their lives as thousands were expected to be killed had the invasion occurred. (Courtesy of Rosena McConica.)

SMALL-TOWN BROTHERS. Santa Paula residents Wayne Harvey (left) and Roger Harvey (right) both served as pilots for the Army Air Corps during World War II. Wayne was a first lieutenant with the 400th Bomb Group and completed 50 missions in the South Pacific. Roger was a first lieutenant with the 398th Bomb Group and completed 32 missions in Europe. (Courtesy of Roger Harvey.)

T.C. Robinson, 1945. Santa Paula resident Robinson (far right) was inducted into the Army on November 11, 1942, and he served with the 91st Infantry, Fifth Army, throughout Italy. He was discharged on October 8, 1945. (Courtesy of Fred Robinson.)

Roger Robinson, 1968. The youngest Robinson brother was drafted into the Army in May 1967. He was sent to combat in Vietnam in October 1967 and was assigned to C Company, 1st Battalion, 5th Infantry, 25th Division. Among Robinson's combat experiences was the Tet Offensive in January 1968. (Courtesy of Fred Robinson.)

TWINS. Floyd and Lloyd Robinson, also brothers to Roger and T.C. Robinson, enlisted in the Army in October 1950. Floyd was sent to Korea while Lloyd was sent to Germany. They were initially promised that they would not be separated and were eventually reunited to finish their service on active duty in Germany. Here, they are photographed at Fort Benning, Georgia, in 1950. (Courtesy of Fred Robinson.)

ARTHUR TARIN. The Ventura High School graduate (right) enlisted in the Army Air Corps on June 21, 1941. He was sent to combat in Africa and Sicily and wrote home to his parents about how much he enjoyed Sicily and all the friends he met. While leaving on a mission in Sicily on July 6, 1944, just days before his 22nd birthday, the aircraft carrying Tarin and his crew crashed, killing all on board. (Courtesy of Mary Lou Roberts.)

ARMANDO TARIN. One of three Tarin brothers to serve, Armando was drafted into the Army in March 1944. In September 1944, he was taken as a POW by the Germans and was not liberated until April 1945. (Courtesy of Mary Lou Roberts.)

JOHN TARIN. A younger Tarin brother, John, served in Korea. Here, he is pictured on the left in Fairbanks, Alaska, in 1951. (Courtesy of Mary Lou Roberts.)

RUBEN RENTERIA. Oxnard resident Renteria was a marine from 1951 to 1954. He served in Korea and was wounded on March 19, 1953, while in combat. (Courtesy of Rachel Beas.)

MANUEL RENTERIA. Manuel was Ruben's brother and served in the Army as a radioman in Korea. He was inducted in 1951 and was discharged in 1954. (Courtesy of Rachel Beas.)

RAUL REYES. Santa Paula resident Reyes was the eldest of three brothers to serve in the military, and he served in the Army Air Corps during World War II. (Courtesy of Debbie Lopez.)

111

MANUEL REYES. Manuel was the younger brother of Raul, and he enlisted in the Navy when he was just 16 years old on March 3, 1942. He lied about his birth year and had to get his mother to sign for him. But the young seaman felt that it was important for him to serve his country. (Courtesy of Debbie Lopez.)

JULIAN REYES. Julian was the youngest of the three Reyes brothers to serve and was a reconnaissance photographer for the Army during the Korean War. (Courtesy of Debbie Lopez.)

ALFREDO AND ALFONSO GONZALEZ. Oxnard residents Alfredo and Alfonso Gonzales were brothers who served in the Army during the Korean War. Alfredo arrived in South Korea in the spring of 1951 and was attached to the 25th Signal Corps, 25th Division. He worked as a teletype operator. Alfonso arrived in the summer of 1951 and was assigned to the Army Postal Service in Suwon, approximately 20 miles from Seoul. Here, the brothers are pictured outside of the message center near Uijongbu, South Korea. (Courtesy of Alfredo Gonzalez.)

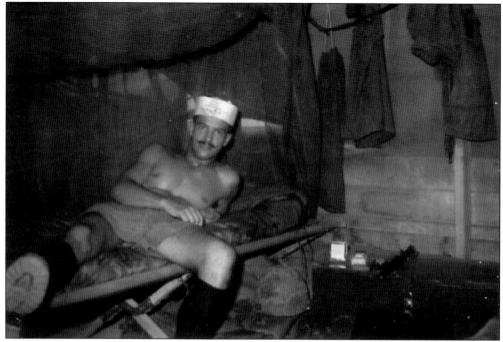

LYNDON CLIFFORD BENSEN JR. Former Santa Paula resident Bensen was a decorated Vietnam veteran. In addition, he was noted to have been an alternate for the US gymnastics team and 1960 Olympic Games. (Courtesy of Kay Davison-Culpepper.)

RICHARD LEE BENSEN. Richard was the brother of Lyndon Bensen and graduated from Santa Paula High School in 1964. Soon after, he enlisted in the Army and served tours in Germany and Vietnam. He returned to the United States in 1967. (Courtesy of Kay Davison-Culpepper.)

Stanley Kimzey. Former Ventura resident Kimzey served in the Coast Guard during World War II, completing patrols along the California coast from San Diego to Lompoc. Here, he is pictured with his wife, Cleila. (Courtesy of Cleila Dougherty.)

Roger Kimzey. Pictured here is Stanley's son Roger who was a jet mechanic for the Air Force during the Vietnam War. He served at Lackland Air Force Base and Sheppard Air Force Base, which are both located in Texas. He also served at George Air Force Base in Victorville, California. (Courtesy of Cleila Dougherty.)

ED PRIETO

EDWARD PRIETO. Former Santa Paula resident Prieto served in the Pacific as a marine during World War II. (Courtesy of Pete Prieto.)

PETE PRIETO. Pictured here is Edward's brother Pete who enlisted as a marine on December 11, 1942. He was sent first to New Zealand, where he joined the 2nd Marine Division, and then he went on to fight in the Battle of Tarawa in November 1943. He went on to also fight in Okinawa. Pete's brother Richard also served as a soldier in Italy. (Courtesy of Pete Prieto.)

HARLAN WAYNE FOOTE. Former Ventura resident Foote (left) enlisted in the Navy during World War II. He had always been interested in planes. Because he had taken flying lessons at Santa Paula Airport, he was sent to the airfield at Los Alamitos to train in Navy aviation. Here, he is pictured aboard the USS *Hornet* with Navy friends in 1945. Foote is a recipient of the Navy Cross. (Courtesy of Shelly Foote.)

DONALD FOOTE. Prior to the beginning of World War II, Donald Foote worked in aviation at North American Aviation in Los Angeles, which is where LAX is currently located. Because the company assisted with the war effort, Foote was given a deferment until the end of the war when he was drafted. Foote served in the South Pacific. Here, he is pictured at Tenney Park in Madison, Wisconsin, with his wife, Jane. (Courtesy of Shelly Foote.)

JOE VILLA. Santa Paula resident Villa was inducted into the Army in February 1943, and he served as an artillery mechanic in heavy antiaircraft at Camp Haan in Riverside, California. He was discharged from active duty on July 6, 1945. (Courtesy of Robert and Carol Villa.)

FRANK VILLA. Frank Villa is the older brother to Joe and entered active duty on April 7, 1942. He served under Lt. Col. James Doolittle as an automotive equipment mechanic in the Army Air Corps. He was discharged on October 25, 1945. (Courtesy of Robert and Carol Villa.)

GRADY WILLARD BREWER. Former Santa Paula resident Brewer served as a member of the National Guard during World War II.

DONALD GRADY BREWER. Donald is the son of Grady Brewer, and here, the former marine is shown in a portrait that was taken in 1959.

SIMON MELENDEZ. Former Saticoy resident Melendez was inducted into the Army on February 9, 1951. He served active duty in combat in the Battle of Bloody Ridge and the Battle of Heartbreak Ridge. On October 11, 1951, he received a Purple Heart for wounds he received behind enemy lines. (Courtesy of Mariza Sullivan.)

BROTHERS REUNITED. Simon Melendez (left) and Raymond Melendez (right) are pictured in a newspaper clipping marking their reunion in Korea, after Raymond was able to secure a three-day pass for the visit. At the time, Raymond had been in Korea for six months while Simon was there for seven months. (Courtesy of Mariza Sullivan.)

REUNION IN KOREA—The Melendez brothers, Simon (left) and Raymond, of Saticoy get together for visit in Korea.

Two Saticoy Brothers Reunited For Three-Day Visit in Korea

Despite the rigors of warfare in Korea two Saticoy brothers found time to hold a three-day reunion at an unnamed camp near the front last month.

Simon Melendez, 21 and brother Raymond, 23, held their impromptu family gathering when Ray wrangled a three-day pass to make the 100-mile trip. They are the sons of Mr. and Mrs. Ref-

uglo Melendez, Saticoy. The pair didn't know where either boy was stationed.

A third member of the family brother-in-law Tony Ayala, Santa Paula, was stationed about 50 miles away but was unable to get in on the happy occasion.

Raymond, a paratrooper, has been in Korea for six months. His brother has been there for seven months and has been wounded

Five

THE ULTIMATE SACRIFICE

NEWLYWEDS. Don Buchanan is pictured with his new bride, Joyce, on their wedding day on September 2, 1951. The Ventura resident was sent to Korea on December 15, 1951. He was killed by direct mortar on July 5, 1952, which was a little more than 10 months after this photograph was taken. He had been a member of Company D, 2nd Battalion, 5th Marines, 1st Marine Division. (Courtesy of Joyce Cantrell.)

JOE AVENDANO. On the night of January 23, 1944, a volunteer crew of six, including Capt. Joe Avendano of Santa Paula, boarded a B-24 to test a radar system and the plane's equipment for an upcoming mission. Comdr. John Roche was communicating with Avendano throughout the test when the plane suddenly began descending and crashed, causing a massive explosion and killing the entire crew. (Courtesy of Joe and Phyllis Duran.)

JOHN CONTRERAS. On January 21, 1968, the 18-year-old Contreras was caught in heavy combat near Khe Sanh, Vietnam, and was killed by enemy fire. In an online post, fellow comrade Earl Kerns, whose feet were caught in wire during the battle, recalled a few moments from the Battle of Khe Sanh. He thanked Contreras for freeing him and saving his life while Contreras sacrificed his own on Hill 861. (Courtesy of Julio Contreras.)

PFC. JOHN CONTRERAS
Killed in Vietnam

Carpinteria Youth Killed In Viet War

Marine Pfc. John Contreras, 18, of Carpinteria, was killed in action Monday in Vietnam.

His mother, Mrs. Ruben Gonzales, of 1347 Cramer Rd., Carpinteria, was notified by the Marine Corps that Pfc. Contreras had been killed.

He was serving with the 26th Marines, Third Battalion, at Khe Sanh.

He enlisted last June after completing his junior year at Carpinteria High School.

Pfc. Contreras is survived by a sister, Mrs. Michael (Amelia) Lopez of Santa Barbara; three brothers in Carpinteria, David, Victor and Manuel; a brother on duty with the 1st Marine Air Wing in Vietnam, Cpl. Charles Gonzales; another brother, Julio, who received his honorable discharge last month and is back in Santa Barbara from Vietnam after service with the 27th Marines, 2nd Bn.; a grandmother, Mrs. Victoria Dalgado, the widow of Victoriano Dalgado, and an aunt, Miss Vera Dalgado of Summerland.

Funeral services will be announced when the body is returned here from Vietnam.

ISABEL PRIETO. Santa Paula resident Prieto served as a marine during World War II and was killed during the invasion of Bougainville in 1943. (Courtesy of Pete Prieto.)

RAMON PRIETO. Ramon was the brother of Isabel and a paratrooper who was killed in France during the D-Day invasion in June 1944. Like Isabel, Ramon was eventually brought home and buried at the Pierce-Brothers Santa Paula Cemetery. (Courtesy of Pete Prieto.)

SANTA PAULA FLIER KILLED

First Lt. Edwin Pinkerton, Santa Paula Mustang pilot, was killed in action in France on Aug. 7, the war department has informed his widow, Helen Pinkerton of Saticoy.

No details were given, but Mrs. Pinkerton was informed that a letter was to follow the death message. A veteran of at least 32 combat missions. Lt. Pinkerton earlier had been reported as missing in action.

Holder of the Air Medal and three oak leaf clusters and a presidential unit citation, the Santa Paula flier was credited with shooting down at least one Nazi plane. He served with the Ninth air force.

Before going overseas, Lt. Pinkerton was an AAF instructor for two years at Luke field, Ariz. A graduate of Santa Paula high school and the University of California at Davis, he also attended Ventura junior college.

Besides his widow, the flier is survived by a 10-months-old son, Kurt Kimball Pinkerton, and his mother, Mrs. W. J. Pinkerton, Santa Paula.

DOYLE TORY. Former Santa Paula resident Tory (middle) enlisted in the Navy in 1941 and spent four years in active service. He continued his service after World War II as a member of the reserves. On May 22, 1961, during a reserve training program, Tory was killed when the S2F antisubmarine plane he was flying crashed on a remote portion of San Clemente Island, California. (Courtesy of Jeri Tory Conklin.)

EDWIN PINKERTON. Santa Paula resident Pinkerton was featured in this newspaper clipping after he was killed while flying on a mission over France on August 7, 1944. Pinkerton was a veteran of more than 32 missions as a Mustang pilot and served with the Ninth Air Force. He left behind his wife and his 10-month-old son. (Courtesy of Joe Jauregui.)

SAD, BUT PROUD BROTHERS—The three brothers of Pfc. Edward Chavez read the newspaper account of how he died a hero in Viet Nam. From left are Victor, David and Frank.

EDDIE CHAVEZ. Santa Paula resident Chavez was sent to Vietnam on October 27, 1966. On November 21, less than a month after his arrival, the 20-year-old soldier was killed by hostile fire in South Vietnam. Pictured from left to right are his brothers Victor, David, and Frank in a newspaper clipping that shows them learning of their brother's heroic death. Chavez was one of 21 soldiers from the 1st Air Cavalry Division that held back a battalion of 400 North Vietnamese for four hours. After they were overpowered, only three of the 21 soldiers survived. (Courtesy of Mark Aguirre.)

JIMMY CAVENDER. Jimmy was the younger Cavender brother to serve during Vietnam and was drafted into the Army in 1967. After months of training and a promotion to sergeant, Cavender decided to become a helicopter pilot. On November 4, 1969, while flying a Huey helicopter en route to Nha-Trang, Vietnam, the aircraft crashed because of bad weather, which killed the entire crew. Their bodies were never recovered. Cavender was only 20 years old. (Courtesy of James Cavender.)

WILLARD PAYNE. Payne is pictured here during his senior year at Santa Paula High School. His tour in Vietnam began on August 24, 1970. On August 10, 1971, nearly a year after first arriving, the 27-year-old soldier was killed from injuries that were sustained in South Vietnam. It was just two weeks before he was scheduled to return home. (Courtesy of Joe Jauregui.)

MAX VASQUEZ. Santa Paula resident Vasquez was a medic with the 101st Airborne Division. He was drafted into the Army in the spring of 1965 and was sent to Vietnam on May 3, 1966. On June 10, just over a month after his arrival, Vasquez was killed by hostile fire in South Vietnam. (Courtesy of John Vasquez.)

BERNARD MORRIS. Oxnard resident Morris was a member of the 279th Replacement Company, 85th Infantry, during World War II. On February 11, 1945, Morris was killed when the landing ship tank he was aboard was attacked by an enemy submarine. The LST was travelling from Hollandia, New Guinea to the Philippines. (Courtesy of Tommy Morris.)

www.arcadiapublishing.com

M A P   S E A R C H

Discover books about the town where you grew up, the cities where your friends and families live, the town where your parents met, or even that retirement spot you've been dreaming about. Our Web site provides history lovers with exclusive deals, advanced notification about new titles, e-mail alerts of author events, and much more.

Arcadia Publishing, the leading local history publisher in the United States, is committed to making history accessible and meaningful through publishing books that celebrate and preserve the heritage of America's people and places. Consistent with our mission to preserve history on a local level, this book was printed in South Carolina on American-made paper and manufactured entirely in the United States.

This book carries the accredited Forest Stewardship Council (FSC) label and is printed on 100 percent FSC-certified paper. Products carrying the FSC label are independently certified to assure consumers that they come from forests that are managed to meet the social, economic, and ecological needs of present and future generations.

FSC

Mixed Sources
Product group from well-managed forests and other controlled sources

Cert no. SW-COC-001530
www.fsc.org
© 1996 Forest Stewardship Council

Find *Your* Place in History.